A Benjamin Blog
and his Inquisitive Dog
Investigation

Exploring Rivers

Anita Ganeri

Heinemann
LIBRARY

Chicago, Illinois

To contact Capstone Global Library please
phone 800-747-4992, or visit our web site,
www.capstonepub.com

Edited by Dan Nunn, Rebecca Rissman, and Helen
Cox Cannons
Designed by Joanna Hinton-Malivoire
Original illustrations © Capstone Global Library Ltd
Illustrated by Sernur ISIK
Picture research by Mica Brancic
Production by Helen McCreath
Originated by Capstone Global Library Ltd

**Library of Congress Cataloging-in-Publication
Data**
Ganeri, Anita, 1961- author.
 Exploring rivers : a Benjamin Blog and his
inquisitive dog investigation / Anita Ganeri.
    pages cm.—(Exploring habitats, with Benjamin
Blog and his inquisitive dog)
 Includes bibliographical references and index.
 ISBN 978-1-4329-8775-6 (hb)—ISBN 978-1-4329-
8782-4 (pb) 1. Stream ecology—Juvenile literature.
2. Rivers—Juvenile literature. 3. Stream animals—
Juvenile literature. I. Title.

QH541.5.S7G36 2014
551.48'3—dc23   2013017417

Acknowledgments
The author and publisher are grateful to the
following for permission to reproduce copyright
material: Corbis p. 20 (© Eric and David Hosking);
eoimages p. 25 (NASA); FLPA p. 29 top (Mark
Sisson); Getty Images pp. 6 (DEA/G. COZZI), 16
(Ritterbach Ritterbach), 18 (Farhana Jenny), 22
(© Peter Walton Photography); Naturepl.com p.
7 (© Jim Clare); Photoshot p. 27 (© NHPA/Nigel
Hicks); Robert Harding World Imagery p. 9 (Ben
Pipe Photography/Robert Hard); Shutterstock
pp. 4 (© Josef Hanus), 5 (© feiyuezhangjie), 8 (©
atm2003), 10 (© Chawalit S.), 11 (© LysFoto), 14
(© Porojnicu Stelian), 17 (© David Hughes), 23
(© LehaKoK); SuperStock pp. 12 (Hemis.fr), 13
(Wolfgang Kaehler), 15 (Marka), 19 (age fotostock/
Martin Zwick), 21 (Minden Pictures/Ingo Arndt), 24
(Hemis.fr), 26 (imagebroker.net), 29 bottom (age
fotostock/Martin Zwick).

Cover photograph of a river in the Altai Mountains,
Russia, reproduced with permission of Shutterstock
(© straga).

We would like to thank Michael Bright for his
invaluable help in the preparation of this book.

Every effort has been made to contact copyright
holders of any material reproduced in this book.
Any omissions will be rectified in subsequent
printings if notice is given to the publisher.

All the Internet addresses (URLs) given in this
book were valid at the time of going to press.
However, due to the dynamic nature of the
Internet, some addresses may have changed,
or sites may have changed or ceased to exist
since publication. While the author and publisher
regret any inconvenience this may cause readers,
no responsibility for any such changes can be
accepted by either the author or the publisher.

Some words are shown in bold, **like this**. You can find
out what they mean by looking in the glossary.

Contents

Exploring Rivers!

Hello! My name's Benjamin Blog and this is Barko Polo, my **inquisitive** dog. (He's named after the ancient ace explorer **Marco Polo**.) We have just returned from our latest adventure—exploring rivers around the world. We put this book together from some of the blog posts we wrote on the way.

BARKO'S BLOG-TASTIC RIVER FACTS

Rivers flow through almost every country in the world. They sweep down from mountains and across **plains**, carrying water to the sea. This is the Yulong River in China.

Rushing River

Posted by: Ben Blog | February 28 at 9:15 a.m.

We started our trip here on Lake Victoria in East Africa. It is the main **source** of the Nile River, the world's longest river. It flows out of the lake as a stream. The source is the place where a river starts. Other rivers start off as mountain **springs** or flow from **glaciers**.

BARKO'S BLOG-TASTIC RIVER FACTS

The icy Gangotri Glacier is high up in the Himalayas in India. In spring and summer, the end of the glacier melts and starts off a stream that becomes the Ganges River.

Canyon Carving

Posted by: Ben Blog | April 9 at 2:18 p.m.

At the start, a river flows fast and carries along boulders, pebbles, and sand. These grind away at the river bed, carving out valleys and **canyons**. This is the Grand Canyon in the United States. It was carved out by the Colorado River and is 277 miles (446 kilometers) long and 1 mile (1½ kilometers) deep in places.

BARKO'S BLOG-TASTIC RIVER FACTS

In the mountains, rivers carve out steep-sided, V-shaped valleys, like this one in Nepal. It was made by the Dudh Kosi River that flows down Mount Everest.

Wonderful Waterfalls

We are visiting Niagara Falls on the border between Canada and the United States. This is probably the world's most famous waterfall, so I took lots of photos. Waterfalls form when a river flows over a shelf of hard rock, eating away at the soft rock underneath.

BARKO'S BLOG-TASTIC RIVER FACTS

Angel Falls in Venezuela is the tallest waterfall in the world. Here, the Churun River plunges 3,212 feet (979 meters) down Devil's Mountain. What an awesome sight!

Winding Rivers

Our last day in the United States was spent on the mighty Mississippi River. I wanted to see its **meanders**. Here's a photo I took from a helicopter. Meanders are great loops or bends made as the river swings from side to side. This happens when the river winds its way slowly across flat land.

BARKO'S BLOG-TASTIC RIVER FACTS

As a river flows along, other streams flow into it. They are called **tributaries**. Some tributaries are big enough to count as rivers. This is the Maranon River, a tributary of the Amazon River.

13

Running Away to Sea

Posted by: Ben Blog | June 24 at 7:09 a.m.

Today we are by the Black Sea in Romania. Here, the Danube River dumps its load of rocks and sand before it flows into the sea. It forms a fan-shaped area of new land, called a **delta**. The Danube Delta is huge, and it is home to some amazing animals, such as these pelicans.

BARKO'S BLOG-TASTIC RIVER FACTS

Some rivers do not flow into the sea. The Okavango River flows into the Kalahari Desert in Botswana. In the rainy season, it's full of wildlife—like these hippopotamuses!

Riverside Gardens

Posted by: Ben Blog | July 26 at 8:32 a.m.

Plenty of plants live on rivers, but these water lilies on the Amazon River are the biggest that I have ever seen. Their enormous pads float on the surface and can grow 8 feet (2.5 meters) across. They are supposed to be strong enough for humans to sit on, so I'm going to try it!

Next stop on our trip was the Sundarbans. It is a massive forest of mangrove trees that grows across the **delta** of the Ganges and Brahmaputra Rivers in India and Bangladesh. Mangrove trees have roots that sprout from their trunks. These fix the trees firmly in the mud.

BARKO'S BLOG-TASTIC RIVER FACTS

These river red gum trees grow along the banks of rivers in Australia. Their branches fall into the water and make useful shelters for fish. Animals also eat their fallen leaves.

19

Watery Wildlife

Posted by: Ben Blog | August 12 at 2:22 p.m.

Rivers are home to some amazing animals. I spotted these torrent ducks on the Urubamba River, in the Andes Mountains. The fast-flowing water is dangerous, but the ducks are strong swimmers and divers. They also have claws on their feet to grip the slippery rocks.

BARKO'S BLOG-TASTIC RIVER FACTS

Otters have **streamlined** bodies and webbed paws for swimming after their **prey** of fish. They also have thick, waterproof fur to keep them dry and warm. Lucky otters—dogs just get wet!

Back in Australia, we went out on the river with some scientists who are studying saltwater crocodiles. These massive reptiles lie in the water, looking like logs. Then they attack fish and other animals that come to the river for a drink. I took a photo of this one before it tried to snap me!

BARKO'S BLOG-TASTIC RIVER FACTS

Piranhas are small fish from South America. They are famous for their razor-sharp teeth. Some are fierce meat-eaters, but some only eat fruit and seeds that fall into the water.

Record-Breaking River

Posted by: Ben Blog | September 6 at 6:13 p.m.

Next we headed to Egypt to visit my favorite river—the Nile. It is 4,160 miles (6,695 kilometers) long, the longest river in the world. The ancient Egyptians used to live on the banks of the Nile. You can still see their temples and pyramids when you're taking a relaxing **felucca** ride.

felucca

Mediterranean Sea

Nile Delta

Red Sea

source of river

BARKO'S BLOG-TASTIC RIVER FACTS
The Nile River flows mainly from Lake Victoria, across Africa, and into the Mediterranean Sea. Here, it forms a huge delta that has very rich soil for growing crops.

Ruined Rivers

Posted by: Ben Blog | October 13 at 1:56 p.m.

Last stop on our trip was the Rhine River in Germany. For centuries, this river has been used for transportation, and many factories were built on its banks. But it has also been used as a dumping ground for trash, chemicals, and **sewage**. Luckily, the clean-up has begun.

BARKO'S BLOG-TASTIC RIVER FACTS

The Yangtze river dolphin became **extinct** in 2006. It was only found in a few rivers in China, including the Yangtze River, one of the busiest and dirtiest rivers in the world.

Rushing Rivers Explorer Quiz

If you are planning your own river expedition, you need to be prepared. Find out how much you know about rushing rivers with our quick quiz.

1. Where does the Nile River start?
a) Lake Nasser
b) Lake Victoria
c) Lake Superior

2. Which is the tallest waterfall?
a) Niagara
b) Victoria
c) Angel

3. What is a **meander**?
a) bend in a river
b) small river
c) river plant

4. Where does the Okavango River end?
a) in the sea
b) in the desert
c) in the mountains

5. What do piranhas eat?
a) meat
b) fruit
c) seeds

6. Which is the longest river?
a) Nile
b) Amazon
c) Yangtze

7. What is this?

8. What is this?

Glossary

canyon long, deep cut in Earth's surface

delta fan-shaped piece of new land that builds up where a river flows into the sea

extinct animal or plant that has died out forever

felucca sailing boat on the Nile River

glacier huge river of ice that flows down a mountainside

inquisitive interested in learning about the world

Marco Polo explorer who lived from about 1254 to 1324. He traveled from Italy to China.

meander huge bend or loop in a river

plain large, flat stretch of land

prey animals that are hunted and eaten by other animals

sewage waste from humans and animals

source place where a river begins

spring water that flows up from underground

streamlined smooth, tube-shaped. An otter's body is streamlined to allow easy movement through water.

tributary smaller stream that flows into a main river

Find Out More

Books

Gray, Leon. *Rivers* (Geography Wise). New York: Rosen, 2011.

Parker, Steve. *Eyewitness Pond and River.* New York: DK Publishing, 2011.

Throp, Claire. *The Nile River* (Explorer Tales). Chicago: Raintree, 2013.

Waldron, Melanie. *Rivers* (Habitat Survival). Chicago: Raintree, 2013.

Web Sites

FactHound offers a safe, fun way to find Internet sites related to this book. All of the sites on FactHound have been researched by our staff.

Here's all you do:
Visit www.facthound.com
Type in this code: 9781432987756

Index